Faces of America

PHOTOGRAPHED AND WRITTEN BY

EILEEN M. FOTI

To order additional copies of this book, contact:
Xlibris
844-714-8691
www.Xlibris.com
Orders@Xlibris.com

ISBN: Softcover   978-1-6698-1168-8
        Hardcover   978-1-6698-1167-1
        EBook   978-1-6698-1166-4

Library of Congress Control Number: 2022903602

Print information available on the last page

Rev. date: 05/27/2022

OTHER BOOKS BY THE AUTHOR

DRUGS, Gems, and Murder
To Catch a Rat
......And Then the Chase
Up in Flames
Some Vacation!

CHILDREN'S BOOKS

Butterflies, Beasties, Blooms, Etc.
The Adventure of the Wee Cave People
Puppy Love
The Goslings of Thorpe Village
Mousey And The Fireman
Yes, There Are Name Other Than Rover!
Rose Fairies
Bunny and the Rainbow

DEDICATION

This book is for all the hard working Americans
who go about their lives, achieving more than they
are aware of, living productive lives, and helping
wherever they can. May God reward your efforts!

AUTHOR'S NOTE

I would like to thank each and every
person for contributing, and allowing,
their photo to appear in this book.

You are all unique in your own way!

FACES OF AMERICA

Our Constitution starts with the words, "We the people of the United States...."

It doesn't say certain people of the United States, it says, "We the people.", meaning all people living in the United States of America, we are one country, and one people. We do not all look the same. Our features may be different, our accent may be different, our thinking may be different, our beliefs may vary, however we are all Americans!

In our own way, we have pride for our country. We don't all agree with each other on many topics, but we do stick together, when threatened we will come to the aid of our fellow American. In terrible times we will be there for each other; whether it be offering aid for a sick friend, or a handout when a family member is in need.

This is a book of portraits of Americans. As you can see, all are different, but all are the same, all are Americans!

HELEN ACHESON

Eileen M. Foti

LOUISE LANGAN

HELEN SCHWARZLER

America is made up of millions of people, no two are really alike. However, we all love our families, and for the most part, we are law bidding people.

As different as we are, we are also, in many ways, the same. Who doesn't love a good cooked meal! A great film, then eating pizza after it! A day at the beach, or a walk through the woods!

The simple things we all do every day makes us more alike than not. We pride ourselves by doing a good job at work, or at home, or at play. Whatever the job may be, is important to the one doing it. Yes, we will all do, even the same job differently.

We are people of all walks of life. We groom dogs, we deliver babies, we build highways, and bridges, we scale mountains, because they are there, we teach school, we are religious, we are not religious, we believe or don't believe. We are free as Americans to lead or own lives, even though or neighbors may do it in another way.

VIRGINIA McDONALD

JUDITH McELLIGOTT

JOHNNY MAZARIEGO

When we are sick and need a transfusion, we are grateful to the person who donated the blood. We do not ask who donated the blood, we are just happy to get it. When we come down to it, people help people in more ways than not. We may not all agree with each other, but we do need each other! People supply other people with organs, and all sorts of transplants. Mostly, we are made the same, with different DNA, but we still can help when needed.

SHELLDON MORGAN

Eileen M. Foti

ANGELA UMANA

We are nurses, helping to keep us alive, we are doctors, operating and treating the injured or sick, we are policemen trying to keep us safe, we are cab drivers chauffeuring us around busy city streets, we are ice cream vendors making kids smile while serving them drippy cones on a hot summer day. All of us unique in or own way.

Our ambulances are manned with American attendants. We rush others to the hospital regardless of their color or ethnicity. We look out for each other. We are there whenever the need.

JILL LEDERER

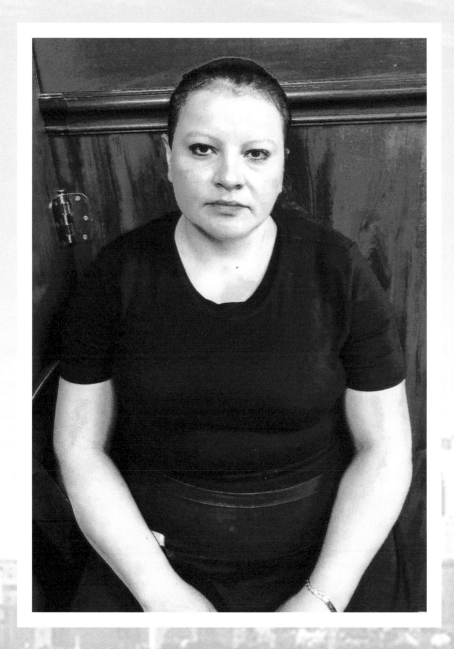

REYNA GUILLEN

So now the world is experiencing a pandemic. It is rolling over the world like a thick, threateningly, murderous fog. Thousands of Americans have lost their lives, millions around the world. Our first responders, nurses, doctors, ambulance drives, EMT people, technicians, all the way to the cleaning staff at the hospitals, have jumped in, with no regard for themselves, to help save lives. They do not care what a sick person looks like, they do not care about his/her name or where he or she came from, they only care enough to help. Many a first responder held the hand of a dying patient in a lonely hospital bed as the family was not allowed in for a last goodbye.

We all needed someone there as we left this world; we didn't care if that person was white or a person of color. Their kindness can never be measured. We may think we are different, and in many ways we are, but we also need others in time of need, and that makes us all the same.

EMMA HOGAN

JACK HOGAN

ADOLFO GUZMAN

Eileen M. Foti

A terrible earthquake has now hit Haiti. Over two thousand people have died, and the number is still going up. American rescue teams are on the way to help. We not only help each other in America, but we also help around the world. Money, food, clothing, and medical supplies are being sent to Haiti. Those who cannot offer physical aid, I'm sure, will offer up a prayer. We can all feel their loss, we can all sympathize with the Haitian people. We all may live dissimilar lives, however, we can relate to one another's pain, we can feel the sorrow, and the tragedy the Haitians are living through.

JENNY UMANA

Eileen M. Foti

DEYSI UMANA

Sometimes just a smile can make somebody's day. Maybe the person receiving that smile is alone, or sick, or just having a really bad day; and then you smile, and for a minute, the world is a little better. That smile didn't cost you anything, but to the receiver it was worth a million! We all can use a smile!

A smile can radiate happiness, acceptance, a sense of belonging. Even if we are rushing along to work, shopping, or anywhere you go in your busy life, a smile will make the journey seem better.

Eileen M. Foti

LIZBETH KALL

NEAL LEIBESBERGER

We are firemen, rushing into burning buildings, regardless of our safety, to rescue people we don't even know. Whatever their color, creed, or nationality, we are there to help and save to the best of our ability. We are brave and adversity brings this bravery forward, without question, we are American Firefighters!

Recently, Ida hit the New York-New Jersey area. The Orangeburg Fire Department rescued people stranded and trapped in their cars along Route 303 in Orangeburg-Blauvelt area. They used motorized row boats to take people from their cars and bring them to safety. Also, at the same time, a train derailed, throwing seven cars off the tracks. One was a tanker filled with gas that could have exploded, thank God it didn't. These brave fire fighters helped to bring everything back to normal – people safe, train back on track!

These fire fighters, of different backgrounds, different ethnicity, different beliefs, came together to help bring their fellow Americans to safety.

Americans stick together when it counts!

BRETT WOLOWITZ

Member of Orangeburg Fire Department

Eileen M. Foti

ALFREDO GODINEZ

Member of Orangeburg Fire Department

Not all Americans follow the golden path in life. But that's to be expected. We are all alike in many ways, but not in every way. That's what makes America great! We can live the life we choose, providing we don't hurt others. Our cars are different colors, but most of us have cars, our choice of donuts will vary, but most of us like donuts! Our politics and religion are varied, and that's fine too. We are free to believe what we want to believe. As long as we do not criticize others for they choices, we can all be happy with ours.

Eileen M. Foti

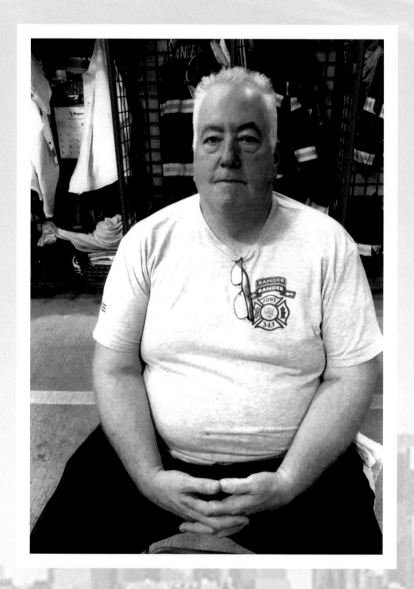

HUGH DUFFY

Member of Orangeburg Fire Department

JIMMY ENGELMAN

Member of Orangeburg Fire Department

JOE SASSANO

Member of Orangeburg Fire Department

Ida has now hit Louisiana. Many homes, and businesses have been destroyed. Some lives were lost, these were Americans, doing nothing wrong, just living their lives. Scenes of the havoc caused by this storm, are being played all over the TV screens. Teams are forming in states, along with Louisiana, to reach out and help the people effected by the hurricane. New York and New Jersey, just to mention two of these states, are sending rescue teams to aid the people of Louisiana. None of the people going down to help know any of the people in Louisiana, however, they can relate to the misery, damage, and heartbreak these people have experienced. Americans stick together!

Ida has also hit New York and New Jersey. Many people have died. Some were trapped in their basement apartments and could not get out as the water poured in and drowned them. Many people tried to help, and did rescue many trapped in the flood water. Americans challenged again and came out fighting!

ELIZABETH WEBER

Member of Orangeburg Fire Department

BRENDAN SCOLLAN

Member of Orangeburg Fire Department

FRANKIE LAVERY

Member of Orangeburg Fire Department

August 30 in American - August 31 in Afghanistan the 20 year of war has ended. After the terrible World Trade bombing, America went after Osama Bin Laden, and established a residence in Afghanistan. Within the last two weeks 120,000 people have been evacuated from Afghanistan. We could not help everyone we wanted too, but we did achieve an amazing number of people brought out, under terrible conditions. We will continue to try to get more Americans home through diplomatic channels. American soldiers, marines, and army personnel, achieved this objective. Everyone pulling together, to help people we do not know! We can all relate to the haunted lives the Afghani's live. We live different lives, but our concern for others is great, and we are there to help all we can. We lost many Americans during this time, and for this we will always be sorry. Nevertheless, the work we did cannot be overlooked. Now the country is back in the hands of the Taliban. We did all we could to improve the lives of many people, people we do not know, but people we reached out to help. We lost thousands of soldiers during this war; 13 lives lost in this effort with a suicide bomber, for this we all mourn. We Americans can hold their heads high knowing all we accomplished, all the aid we offered to Afghanistan, all the people we saved, and hopefully, we will bring out more people who want to leave Afghanistan safely.

Now more trips have been made and more people have escaped. We will probably hear, in the future, about more flights to freedom. We pray for the day everyone is safely home!

Eileen M. Foti

MATT DUFFY

Member of Orangeburg Fire Department

NEIL LYNADY

Member of Orangeburg Fire Department

AARON DUFFY

Member of Orangeburg Fire Department

Americans may not always conform to all the rules and regulations of daily life, however, we do come together when needed. Even if we don't see each other's side, we will pitch in to help in an emergency; we will not strand people in need. Basically, Americans are good people. Sometimes it takes a tragedy to bring out the goodness in people. I have seen, what looked like a hardened person, be kind and generous to a puppy. If we can be kind to an animal, we can be kind to a person. An animal in trouble, for instances, stuck in a pond and in fear of drowning, saved by a stranger who was just walking by. Truly an American thing to do!

JOHN AHLF

Member of Orangeburg Fire Department

BRIAN ARROYO

Member of Orangeburg Fire Department

Even though we are different, the sight of a Christmas tree can be awesome. Even the most hardened person can enjoy the colored lights and beautiful ornaments. The lights remind us of mankind, because we too come in different colors. However, we blend in like the Christmas tree lights when we come together in peace. Or when a child spins a dreidel and hopes for a good result, making part of Hanukkah a little better with each spin. Or celebrating the feast of Kwanza with the pretty colored candles and happy songs.

ROLAND KRASNIQI

Eileen M. Foti

JOSEPH DESNOYERS

GUERLY BRUNO

How many times did we attend a ball game, hot dog in hand, maybe beer in the other hand, cheering our team to victory! We didn't care if the members of the team were like us, same color, same background, same family history, we just cheered the players on. And we had a great time doing it! Our differences brought us together.

FRANK WONG

Eileen M. Foti

SR. ELLENRITA PURCARO, OP

Today we remember 9/11. Two planes carrying many people crashed into the two World Trade Towers. Another one crashed into the Pentagon, and the third crashed at Shanksville, Pennsylvania. The passengers in the Shanksville plane were heroes and brought the plane down before it hit its target. All were lost. Over 3,000 people were lost to this tragedy. Others have since died over the twenty years since that terrible day. Many have died as a result of trying to help rescue other Americans who were trapped in the rubble of the towers. Many forms of cancer have affected these rescuers.

The day of the event, people first thought an accident had happened when the first plane hit the building, but when the second one hit we all knew it was planned. Then we heard about the third plane and we were shocked, we were stunned, we were in disbelief that this could happened to us. As a group of people, American people, we shared this loss as one.

People jumped into action, Rescuers ran into the smoking, burning building to try to bring people out of the carnage. Many who rushed in never came out again. Firemen, policemen, and other citizens all tried to help. No one looked at whatever religion or race a person was, everyone tried to help.

Tug boats, ferries, the Coast Guard, all pitched in and sailed thousands of people across the Hudson River to safety. People pulled together, people helped each other, people cared about each other. That's what Americans do when under critical times. The diversity of the people came together and helped each other out. At a time like this, no one cares about one's background, or politics, or color, or any of a thousand things that make us different from each other. At times likes this we come together and unite as one, we are Americans and we show it!

ANGELA MORFOGEN

SR. MARY McFARLAND, OP

With all our busy lives, we may not have contact with our neighbors. However, if a tragedy befalls them, we are there. We are sympathetic, because tragedy brings common feelings to all of us. Situations may be different, but our emotions run pretty much the same. We are a feeling, compassionate people. On the most part, Americans are not indifferent to others. We see things differently, but we see things!

GLORIA PACE

HENRYI MAZARIEGO

If we reach out to each other, our differences will not all change, but our understanding of each other will. Not everyone is receptive to new ideas, not everyone is open for change, but, when offered, maybe a mutual understand can be achieved. And maybe, after a while, an understanding of each other may occur. If we try each other's shoes on, we may understand why that person is different. We may never want to walk in those shoes again, but we will understand the ones who do!

Eileen M. Foti

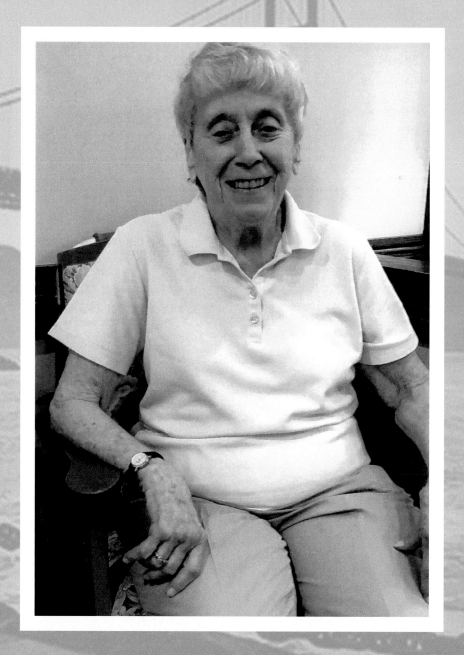

SR. MARY JO LYNCH, OP

Recently at a large sports stadium, a little black and white cat was seen hanging from the bottom of a tier of seats. She was hanging by, what appeared to be the nails of one little paw. The people above the cat tried to reach her, but could not. She was too far down. The people underneath the tier of seats, saw the cat and wanted to help. All eyes were focused on the plight of the cat. For a while the game was secondary; the welfare of the little cat came first. As this "little ball of fur" struggled to get free, a man with an American flag, spread it out, and just in time, caught the falling cat within the Stars and Stripes! The fans went wild as the man retracted the cat from the flag and held her up for all to see. The frightened cat was presented to the cheering crowd, and a little life was saved!

This happened because of the kindness of the American people! They could have looked the other way, and just watched the game, but that would not be the American way, that would not be what we would do, we would always try to help. All of these sports fans, all different in nature, in beliefs, in attitudes, all came together to help save this frightened cat.

Many fans went home after this game with a smile on their faces, to tell their friends not about the game, but about the rescue of the stadium cat!

ANTHONY PIPANI

ANTHONY PRESTIPINO

Eileen M. Foti

SR. MIRIAM CATHERINE NEVINS, OP

A terrible incident happened recently in New York. A mother, carrying a baby in her arms, was run over by a car and dragged into a store. Some policemen, and some civilians, ran into the store and lifted the car off the trapped baby. They didn't question who was under the car, they just acted. This kind of bravery is mirrored over and over, not always getting into the news, but happening just the same.

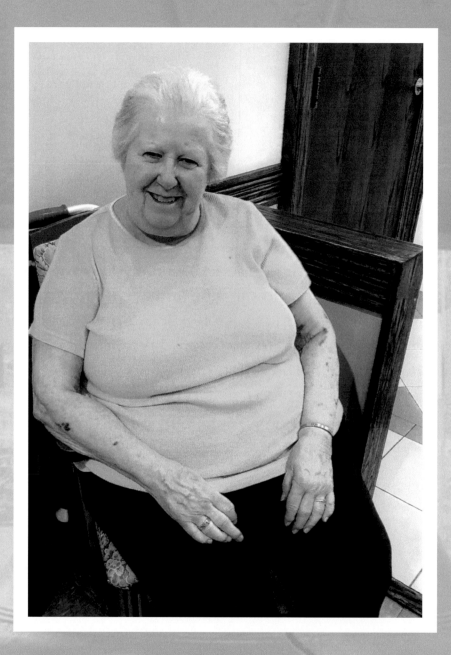

SR. JANE MARRON, OP

CARRIE ADDESSI

SR. MARY ANN COLLINS, OP

Other stories have been told of cars going on fire; people trapped inside and screaming for help. People hearing and seeing this screaming, jumping in to help, pulling the driver out of the burning car, with no fear, for themselves, of being blown up if the car exploded! We are kind hearted Americans! All of us do not know our own strength until we are caught up in a situation where we are needed to act. We only hope to act successfully when the time comes.

Eileen M. Foti

PATRICIA COOKE

VALERIE HOLDER

Every American in this book, has a story to tell. Some stories are really good, while others may not be good. But we each have a story. If we could take the time to listen to the stories of others, how much richer would we be! How much broader would our knowledge of the world be! We would see, even if we see things differently, some of what others say, may resonate with us. Maybe new ground could be traveled in understanding each other. Maybe we'll find out, we all have problems, and we are not so different from each other as we think.

SHARON RUSSO

SEAN RUSSO

Many Americans help out in food kitchens. They serve the people, no matter what nationality, religion, or creed the person may be. They may be different, but people just the same. Hunger is something we can all relate to. Although, some of us never feel the agony of hunger, some of us have all we need to be well fed, however, we can sympathize with those who don't have the means to secure a good meal. We can, and do, show up to help. Some don't help out, but many do, and their kindness is greatly felt!

To see a homeless person come in from the cold, and shyly take a seat at a table, with other people in need, people just trying to stay warm, and trying to fill their bellies with a hot meal, is a joy to behold.

Eileen M. Foti

CLARA McCRIMON

MARIE DESIMONE

I wrote this book because I have heard so many negative things said about Americans, and I know a number of negatives exist, but many good things are overlooked.

Many feelings are shared with each other. We can still be unique, or different, however, in some ways we'll always be the same!

I can see it in the faces of proud Americans showing off their families, sharing a game, telling a story, or just living their lives.

Good people, not out to hurt others, but to live their lives. This sounds simplistic, but when you come down to it, isn't that what we are all trying to do!

We greet our neighbors and friends with a smile, or a handshake. This is a sign of peace. This is a sign of acceptance. This is a sign we care!

We know nothing in life is perfect, a lot of things we'd like to change, and if we go about it peacefully, maybe we can make things better.

We are not naïve, we do not think change will come over night, but if we work towards it, change may happen, possibly so slowly, we may not even see it coming - until it's there!

God Bless America!

Printed in the United States
by Baker & Taylor Publisher Services